D1596032

THE AEGINA
TREASURE

Reynold Higgins

THE AEGINA
TREASURE
An Archaeological
Mystery

A Colonnade Book
Published by British Museum Publications Limited.

8207

To Lucy and Lawrence

With Grandpa's Love

COLONNADE BOOKS
are published by British Museum Publications Ltd
and are offered as contributions to the enjoyment,
study and understanding of art, archaeology and
history.
   The same publishers also produce the official
publications of the British Museum.

© 1979 Reynold Higgins
ISBN 0 7141 8006 8
Published by British Museum Publications Ltd
6 Bedford Square, London WC1B 3RA

DESIGNED BY CRAIG DODD
Set in 11/12 Ehrhardt by Filmtype Services Limited, Scarborough
Reproduction by Keene Engraving Ltd, London
Printed in Great Britain by William Clowes and Sons, Ltd,
Beccles and London.

Contents

Abbreviations

AAA. *Athens Annals of Archaeology*.

AE. *Archaiologiki Ephimeris* (Greek periodical).

BMC FINGER RINGS. F.H. Marshall, *Catalogue of the Finger Rings, Greek, Etruscan and Roman in the British Museum*. London, 1907; reprinted 1968.

BMC JEWELLERY. F.H. Marshall, *Catalogue of the Jewellery, Greek, Etruscan and Roman in the British Museum*. London, 1911; Reprinted 1968.

BOARDMAN, GEMS AND RINGS. John Boardman, *Greek Gems and Finger Rings*. London, 1970.

BSA. *Annual of the British School at Athens*.

CMS. *Corpus der Minoischen und Mykenischen Siegel*.

EVANS, PALACE. A.J. Evans, *The Palace of Minos at Knossos*. 4 vols. London 1921–35.

JHS. *Journal of Hellenic Studies*.

KARO, SCHACHTGRÄBER. G. Karo, *Die Schachtgräber von Mykenai*. Berlin, 1930.

MARINATOS AND HIRMER. S. Marinatos and M. Hirmer, *Crete and Mycenae*. London, 1960.

MYLONAS, GRAVE CIRCLE B. G. Mylonas, *Grave Circle B at Mycenae*. Athens, 1973; in Greek.

PHYLAKOPI. *Excavations at Phylakopi in Melos* (Society for the Promotion of Hellenic Studies, Supp. Paper no. 4, 1904).

SEAGER, MOCHLOS. R.B. Seager, *Explorations in the island of Mochlos*. Boston and New York, 1912.

XANTHOUDIDES. S.A. Xanthoudides, *Vaulted Tombs of Mesara*. London, 1924.

Preface

This book is an updated version of an article which I published over twenty years ago in the *Annual of the British School at Athens* for 1957. It is also an attempt to introduce the story to a wider public, for it is a good story, of more than specialist interest.

Much water has flowed under the bridges since that article was written, and whilst my views as to the date of the Aegina Treasure remain unshaken, my conclusions as to the circumstances of its discovery must be radically modified.

The help of many friends and colleagues was acknowledged in my original article, and I thank them again. For this version I am indebted to yet more friends: Mrs Eugenia Papaleonardou introduced me to Mr George Brown at Aegina in 1959. Mr Michel Emmanuel renewed my interest in the subject and gave me much valuable information; I will always remember that happy day on Aegina in May 1977 with Mr and Mrs Emmanuel and their family. Mrs Stella Xeflouda gave me the benefit of her wide knowledge of Aegina's past and Miss Penny Mountjoy and Dr Stefan Hiller gave me information about the Kamares sherds from Kolonna. For permission to publish the sherds I am indebted to Professor Hans Walter. The photograph of the Thera fresco was taken by Lyvia Morgan Brown and is published by permission of Dr Christos Doumas. Mr John Buxton taught me about owls and Mr Andrew Oddy gave me helpful advice on goldsmith's methods. For help with photos I am indebted to Professor John Boardman, Professor Nicolas Coldstream, Dr Stefan Hiller and Mr Andrew Oddy.

I would like to thank my wife and my daughter Jenny (Mrs P.G. Hay) for reading the manuscript and making many helpful suggestions, all of which I have adopted. Jenny also typed the manuscript for me with uncanny skill, most of it several times. Mrs G.D. March is responsible for the line-drawings and the maps; she too has my grateful thanks. Finally, my thanks are due to Mr Peter Clayton for improving my text and helping me enormously with the illustrations.

1 Map of the Eastern Mediterranean, showing the places in which this story is set.
2 Map of the island of Aegina. The principal city, and port, of the island has always been on the site of the present town, also known as Aegina.

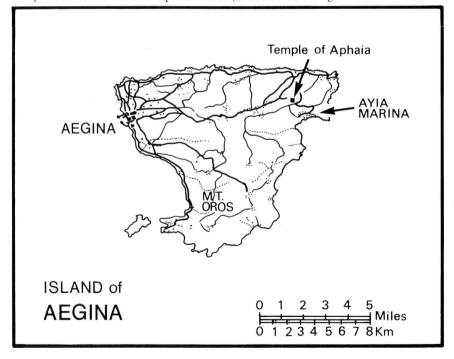

CHAPTER ONE

A Treasure is Bought

In 1891 a rich, beautiful and very perplexing collection of ancient jewellery and gold plate was offered for sale to the British Museum by a Mr George Brown, the agent on the Greek island of Aegina of Cresswell Brothers, a London firm of sponge-dealers. The story, given in confidence to the Museum authorities, was that this collection had been found in a tomb on the island of Aegina.

Aegina is situated some fifteen miles south of Peiraeus, the port of Athens, and about as many miles east of the coast of the Peloponnese (1, 2). This beautiful island is, like so many Greek islands, dry and infertile, and the inhabitants for long lived of necessity by seafaring and manufacturing, at which activities they became extremely successful.

Aegina was prosperous in the Middle and Late Bronze Age, from 2000 to 1100 BC; in the Classical period, from 600 to 400 BC; and under the Venetians, from the thirteenth to the eighteenth century of our era. In 1826 the principal town, also known as Aegina, though today no more than a picturesque port (3), was briefly the capital of a free Greece under the great Kapodistrias (4). Since then the islanders have lived by sponge-fishing, pottery-making, the growing of citrus fruits and pistachio nuts, and (recently) tourism.

The purchase of this rich collection of ancient goldwork was recommended to the Trustees of the British Museum at their meeting on 11 July 1891 by the Keeper of Greek and Roman Antiquities, Mr A.S. Murray. His report is worth quoting in full as being the first recorded reaction of the world of learning to this astonishing discovery.

'Mr Murray has the honour to submit to the Trustees a magnificent collection of gold ornaments, lately found together in a tomb in Aegina. These antiquities are offered for purchase through Messrs Cresswell, 2 Red Lion Square. The price asked is £6,000.

'Mr Murray has endeavoured to get this price reduced but the actual owner of the objects states that his expenditure in connection with the excavation and the personal risks he has run entitle him to a liberal price while the antiquities themselves surpass he believes even those found by Dr Schliemann at Mycenae. He therefore declines to lower his price.

'In some respects this treasure is of higher importance than that found by Dr Schliemann at Mycenae. The workmanship is more advanced and the signs of

3 The harbour and town of modern Aegina. It is today a busy port and a holiday resort for the people of Athens.

indebtedness to Egypt and Assyria more conspicuous. The pendant with a figure holding a swan in each hand has been made under Egyptian influence just as the small ornament representing a hand holding a fruit is evidently an Assyrian idea.

'Like the antiquities of Mycenae this new treasure belongs to an early age of civilisation when the Greeks were being greatly influenced by the older nations of Egypt and Assyria through the medium of the Phoenicians.

'This museum is already rich in the pottery of this early period – obtained from the excavations at Ialyssos in Rhodes. In that respect we are before all other museums except perhaps Athens. But in the matter of gold treasure from this period Athens has hitherto stood alone. Mr Murray earnestly hopes that this will be so no longer. The acquisition of the Aegina treasure would at once place the British Museum in the foremost position as regards this most interesting period in the history of the Greeks.'

The Trustees accepted the recommendation in principle and ordered the Director to approach the Chancellor of the Exchequer for financial assistance.

The Chancellor did not hold out much hope, for lack of available funds; but the prospect improved when the owner reduced his price to £4000. There was again some question of a special grant of £2000 from Parliament; but in the end the Museum was able to find the entire sum from its own resources. And so, on 14 May 1892, the Director of the British Museum reported to the Trustees that the £4000 had been paid to Mr F. Cresswell (on behalf of George Brown) and

4 Aegina town, about 1840, from an old engraving. Though no longer the capital of a free Greece – as it was between 1826 and 1828 – Aegina still retained traces of its former short-lived greatness.

the Treasure was theirs. £4000 was a considerable sum for those days, and should perhaps be multiplied by as much as fifty to bring it into line with modern values; but it reflected the unique richness and importance of the Treasure, which was in many respects quite unlike any other goldwork known from Greek lands. In accordance with accepted practice, neither the vendor's identity nor the purchase price were disclosed. Even the find-spot, in the published Parliamentary Report for 1892, is camouflaged as 'a tomb in one of the Greek islands'.

The Treasure was composed principally of the following objects of gold: three diadems; two pairs of very elaborate earrings; five simple hoops, possibly earrings; a considerable number of beads and pendants of different shapes; two elaborate pendants and part of a third; a pectoral ornament; a bracelet; four inlaid finger-rings; part of a plain finger-ring; fifty-four decorated plaques and a number of plain strips, all for sewing on garments; and a graceful cup with embossed designs. There are also beads and pendants of rock-crystal, amethyst, cornelian, green jasper and lapis lazuli.

Subsequent to its acquisition in 1892, the Treasure was slightly augmented in 1914 by the addition of a few beads which had become separated from it before its arrival in the Museum. Of these, more will be said later.

CHAPTER TWO

How, When and Where?
Investigations, 1893–1957

From the time it appeared in the British Museum, scholars have speculated about this astonishing collection of precious objects. What culture produced it? Where and under what circumstances was it discovered towards the end of the nineteenth century? As will be seen, the two problems are not unconnected, and I think we are now pretty near certainty on both scores; which is the reason for this book.

The first published account was given, with commendable speed, by Dr Arthur Evans, then Keeper of the Ashmolean Museum, Oxford. He was shortly to achieve fame and a knighthood for his discovery and excavation of the fabulous Palace of Minos at Knossos in Crete. But that was still in the future when he published his article entitled 'A Mykenaean Treasure from Aegina' in the *Journal of Hellenic Studies* for 1892–3.

His opening remarks are worth recording, not only for his opinion as to the date of the Treasure, but for his views on the Greek antiquities laws and the results of their application. He says:

'A remarkable Mykenaean gold-find brought to light some years since in the island of Aegina after finding its way into the London market has secured a permanent resting-place in the British Museum. In the interests of archaeological science it must be a matter for rejoicing that our national collection should have received so important an accession in a department of ancient metal-work hitherto almost wholly unrepresented in any museum outside Athens. Opinions may well differ as to the propriety of removing from the soil on which they are found and to which they naturally belong the greater monuments of Classical Antiquity. But in the case of small objects, made themselves for commerce, and free from the same local ties, the considerations, which weigh under other circumstances, lose their validity, while on the other hand the benefits to be derived by students from their partial dispersion are not to be gainsaid. This, it is true, is not the standpoint of the Greek, or, for that matter, of the Turkish Government. But the theory that the present occupants of Greece or the Ottoman possessors of the Eastern Empire are the sole legitimate heirs even of such minor monuments of ancient culture is not likely to commend itself to the outside world. 'Twere hard indeed that not so much as a plaything should come down to us from the cradle of our civilisation.'

'The laws by which not even a coin, or a jewel or a vase is allowed to find its way beyond a certain privileged zone ... inflict a permanent injury on science. The present is a case in point. Certain gold objects, brought into the London market by the ordinary course of trade and that magnetic attraction which brings antiquities to our shores from all parts of the world, are acquired by the British Museum. But the vendor is unable to afford any information as to their provenience, the Museum authorities are naturally no wiser, and though my own investigations point to the fact that the relics in question were found in Aegina, the exact circumstances of the find are at present undiscoverable. It is moreover impossible to say whether other objects of less intrinsic value, such as clay vases, were found with the gold cup and jewellery.'

A detailed stylistic analysis led Evans to the conclusion that the Treasure, whilst exhibiting many Mycenaean features, had been made as late as about 800 BC in Aegina, where he believed Mycenaean traditions to have lingered on long after their demise in much of the Greek world. We now of course know that this view is quite untenable, since the Mycenaean Age has been proved to have ended throughout Greece around 1100 BC; but at the time it was quite a reasonable hypothesis. Later, other, and even more extreme views came to be held, as we shall see.

This is perhaps the moment to explain what is meant by the term 'Mycenaean' (or, as Evans spelled it, 'Mykenaean'). It refers to the brilliant civilization which flourished in Mainland Greece and many of the Greek islands in the Late Bronze Age, between 1600 and 1100 BC. This is the civilization which was dimly remembered by the classical Greeks as their Heroic Age and to which they ascribed such events as the Trojan War. Legend centred it on the city of Mycenae in southern Greece; in 1876 Heinrich Schliemann excavated at that site and discovered the rich tombs of the first kings of Mycenae. Thus legend and archaeology combined in identifying the centre of this culture, and the name Mycenaean inevitably followed.

The subsequent discoveries of Sir Arthur Evans at Knossos from 1900 onwards demonstrated the primacy of the Bronze Age civilization of Crete which he christened Minoan, after Minos, the legendary King of Knossos. This civilization flourished in Crete from about 3000 to 1100 BC and about 1600 BC was largely responsible for the Mycenaean civilization of Mainland Greece, which was eventually to overthrow it.

Very soon after the appearance of his article an event occurred which may well have caused Evans to modify his views as to the late date of the Treasure. He had lamented the fact that no objects of inferior value, such as pottery, had accompanied it or were reported to have been found with it. As if in answer to his prayer, in 1893 Mr J. Cresswell, of Cresswell Brothers, offered to the Ashmolean Museum four Mycenaean vases which were believed to have been found with the Treasure (5, 6). These vases, which were made at different times between 1400 and 1150 BC, were bought for the Ashmolean and were later used by Professor J.L. Myres as evidence for the true Mycenaean date of the Treasure. At the same time the British Museum acquired from the same source two more Mycenaean vases, of 1300-1150 BC, also from Aegina (7).

5 & 6 Four Mycenaean vases believed to have been found in the same tomb as the Treasure. They are now in the Ashmolean Museum, Oxford. Those in illus. 5 were made between 1400 and 1300 BC; those in illus. 6 between 1200 and 1150 BC.

7 Two Mycenaean vases in the British Museum. They too were probably found in the same tomb as the Treasure. That on the left was made between 1200 and 1150 BC, the other between 1300 and 1200 BC.

These we may reasonably assume have the same origin as the Oxford vases, since no other source of Mycenaean pottery was then known on Aegina.

Thus, as early as 1893, there was some evidence, though it was not made public, that the Treasure had been found in an ancient tomb together with Mycenaean pottery made between 1400 and 1150 BC. This rather large time-span need itself cause no disquiet, since Mycenaean tombs were regularly re-used over and over again for burying members of the same family.

Meanwhile the Greek authorities were taking steps to investigate the circumstances of this important discovery. In 1894 a Greek archaeologist, V. Stais, undertook an excavation on the headland north of Aegina town, known, after the one remaining column of a vanished temple, as Cape Kolonna (8). The temple, now ascribed to Apollo, was in those days believed to be that of Aphrodite; a fact which, as will be seen, is relevant to our investigation.

Stais found no traces of any tomb where the Treasure might have been discovered, but believed that such a tomb existed, and was probably located on an eminence to the north of Kolonna. Since, however, he believed (with Evans) that the Treasure was only in part Mycenaean, he was forced to the conclusion that a genuine Mycenaean tomb-group had been supplemented by other objects of a different origin, a common practice amongst sellers of antiquities. He adds, in his report, that the man who sold the Treasure to the British Museum, and claimed to have discovered it, was known to buy anything

8 Cape Kolonna, Aegina. It is named from the sole surviving column of a Greek temple formerly believed to be that of Aphrodite, but now attributed to Apollo. In the foreground are the ruins of the prehistoric city. Left centre is the hexagonal house which belonged to George Brown.

offered to him, whether coming from clandestine excavations or chance discovery.

Rumours soon began to circulate that the Treasure had been found in a tomb in George Brown's vineyard, which was situated on a hill north of Aegina town and east and north-east of Cape Kolonna, known as Windmill Hill (9). An excavation was consequently undertaken in 1904 by another Greek archaeologist, A.D. Keramopoullos, in this vineyard. In the course of his investigations he was fortunate enough to discover four Mycenaean chamber-tombs on the southern slope of the hill. Three proved to be intact, with a large number of vases dating between 1300 and 1200 BC, but no other grave-goods. The fourth had been rifled. No traces of the Treasure, or of anything like it, came to light, but the excavator believed that it might perhaps have been found in the rifled tomb.

Confirmation that Keramopoullos had indeed been operating in the right general area was provided in 1914 by a Miss M. Sinclair, who wrote as follows to the Director of the British Museum:

'In the summer of 1891 Mr George Brown, of Egina, Greece, brought to England, and sold to the British Museum; treasures found in an old tomb of a priestess of the Temple of Venus; sold for £4000. I believe treasures consisting of gold rings,

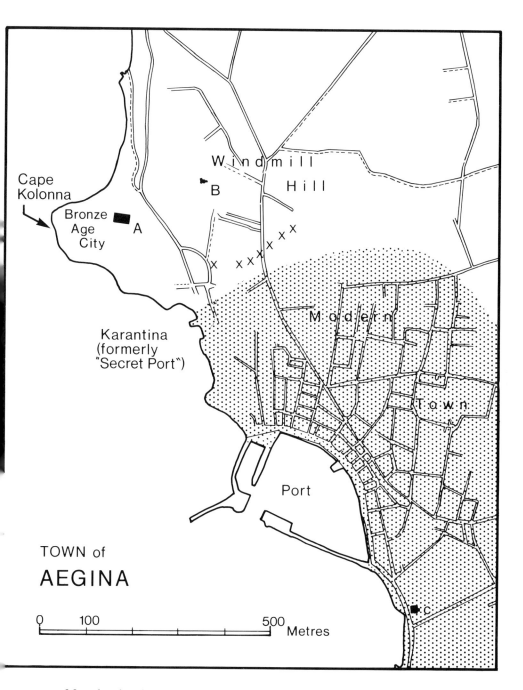

9 Map showing Aegina port and town, Cape Kolonna and Windmill Hill.
A indicates the Temple of Apollo; *B* the Browns' hexagonal house on Windmill Hill; *C* indicates the Browns' principal house, now the Hotel Brown. *X*s denote Mycenaean chamber tombs.

bracelets, pieces of cornelian, jade, and glass beads. At that time I was English governess in their family, coming to England with them and returning with them. Mrs Brown gave me two pieces of cornelian with the carved fingers on it ... A lot of pottery was found in the tomb but not brought to England ... As the things are genuine I wonder if I could sell them, to you or anyone else ....'

The Museum bought the cornelian beads from Miss Sinclair, and in addition eight other pieces of jewellery, all of which clearly belonged to the Aegina Treasure. These pieces have now all been incorporated in it (see illus. 33, for the cornelian beads).

Mention of the pottery is interesting, as supporting Professor Myres's views. The reference to the 'Temple of Venus' is more important, because it indicates that the tomb was situated in the neighbourhood of Cape Kolonna, and very probably therefore, in George Brown's vineyard on Windmill Hill.

A little more light was shed on the origins of the Treasure by an American scholar, J.P. Harland, who was in Aegina in 1920–21 gathering material for a book. In the book, entitled *Prehistoric Aigina*, published in 1925, he states:

'The graves on the hill or high land east and north-east of the site now marked by the remains of the Temple of Aphrodite have yielded a great quantity of typical "Mykenaean", that is, Late Helladic vases ...

'In this connection should be mentioned the "Gold Treasure" from Aigina (now in the British Museum), which I believe came from a Late Helladic grave ... The very place where the "Treasure" was discovered has been pointed out to me by an old inhabitant of Aigina, and the device resorted to by the finder in order to conceal his diggings has also been explained to me. If this evidence is trustworthy – and the camouflage used by the treasure-hunter adds credence to it – then the gold ornaments came from one or possibly two graves. And since this spot is in the midst of the "Mykenaian" or Late Helladic cemetery, it seems to me that the grave and the "Gold Treasure" should be dated in the Late Helladic period, probably in the last decades of the Bronze Age.'

Windmill Hill, certainly. But what of the device by which the finder concealed his digging? We will return to this later.

The next person to show interest in the origins and significance of the Treasure was a Bavarian archaeologist, Dr Gabriel Welter. The connection between Aegina and Bavaria was of long standing. It started in somewhat inauspicious circumstances with the acquisition by the Bavarian Crown Prince Ludwig in 1812 of the sculptures from the Temple of Aphaia in the north-east of the island, and continued with official excavations by the Bavarian Academy of Sciences at the Aphaia and Kolonna sites, which have continued, on and off, up to the present time.

Welter excavated from 1926 till 1940 at and near the Kolonna site, and uncovered much of the Bronze Age settlement on Cape Kolonna itself. Among his finds he records a certain amount of the fine Cretan pottery of 1900–1700 BC known as Kamares Ware; the importance of such pottery on this site will be demonstrated later.

Of more immediate interest is the fact that he found and excavated more Mycenaean tombs on the southern slopes of Windmill Hill, to the east of those excavated by Keramopoullos in 1904 (**9**). He found more chamber-tombs like the earlier ones: rectangular, with a sloping entrance-passage, containing pottery of 1400 to 1200 BC; also some rather earlier cist-graves, of about 1500–1400 BC.

He found no trace of the Treasure. There is, however, little doubt that thanks to the friendly relationship he had built up with the local inhabitants, he had come to learn the true story of its discovery. Possibly, however, in order to protect people still living, he was not inclined to say too much about it. But in his book *Aigina*, published in 1938, he drops a few tantalizing hints. After mentioning the chamber-tombs on Windmill Hill he adds: 'The gold treasure from Aigina which is now in the British Museum was found roughly buried in a hole in the corner of a rifled tomb. It therefore represents a tomb-robber's cache. It is questionable whether the loot actually comes from an Aeginetan cemetery.'

Here was more confirmation of some aspects of the story. But there were clearly even more problems. It looked indeed as if this was no ordinary burial. Why was the Treasure roughly buried in the corner of a Mycenaean tomb? What was the evidence that it had already been rifled? And, most important, why did Welter doubt that the Treasure came from Aegina?

Such was the state of affairs when in 1956, as a junior Assistant Keeper in the Department of Greek and Roman Antiquities in the British Museum, I began to study this fascinating set of goldwork. The more I studied the archaeological evidence, the more I felt that scholars had so far been proceeding on the wrong lines.

By this time, interest in the circumstances surrounding its discovery had died down because with passage of time the trail had grown very cold. Scholars were now studying it, and had been for some time, more from the point of view of its style. Where and when, they were asking, was it made? Unfortunately, they all seemed to come to different conclusions!

Arthur Evans, as we saw above, regarded the Treasure as basically Mycenaean, but made as late as 800 BC, when other influences were making themselves felt in Greek art. The Greek archaeologist V. Stais (convinced, it would seem, by Evans's arguments) preferred to believe that a true Mycenaean tomb-group had been adulterated with alien (and later) elements. F.H. Marshall, who gave the definitive publication in the Departmental *Catalogue of Jewellery* in 1911, saw the Treasure as completely homogeneous and believed that 'a date of 1200–1000 B.C. may serve to indicate the probable position of this treasure at the close of the Mycenaean Age'. Sir John Myres held to the same opinion, which he based on the presence of the Mycenaean vases in Oxford. When I wrote to him, he answered: 'The associated pottery was acquired by Sir Arthur Evans, and is in the Ashmolean Museum ... My own information was from Sir Arthur Evans about the time of its arrival at the Ashmolean.'

Other scholars, however, tended to date the Treasure even later than Evans

10 The ruins of a stone tomb ('Chrysolakkos') at Mallia, North Crete. It was the
communal burial place of royalty and nobles between 1900 and 1600 BC.

had, in the seventh century BC, and one even saw it not as Greek but as
Phoenician. It is possible to sympathize with their views, for which they had
good reasons, without necessarily agreeing with them. But no theory had as yet
accounted for all the facts.

My own investigations led to a new conclusion. It seemed to me that the
non-Mycenaean elements, which had so often proved a stumbling-block, could
be explained not as post-Mycenaean but as pre-Mycenaean. Or, to be more
accurate, I saw the Treasure as uniform in style and therefore all belonging
together; Cretan rather than Mycenaean in origin, and made between 1700 and
1500 BC, at a time when the art of Crete was beginning to penetrate into
mainland Greece, so that it is not always easy for an archaeologist to distinguish
Cretan from Mycenaean work. I also evolved a revolutionary theory as to the
finding-place of the Treasure. If my dating was correct, it was at least three
centuries older than the vases reputedly found with it; older too by as many
centuries than the excavated chamber-tombs on Windmill Hill. It was also, I
thought, Cretan and not Mycenaean. What if Stais was right as to the
commercial morality of George Brown, and Welter was right as to the possibly
non-Aeginetan origin of the Treasure? Could it be that it had been acquired
not in Aegina but in the land where it was made nearly four thousand years
earlier: in Crete? And if so, how and why could this elaborate deception have
been achieved?

I worked out a theory that the Treasure had been acquired in Crete by Brown's sponge-fishers, for sponge-divers from Aegina were known to operate off Crete. E.J.J. Cresswell, in his interesting book, *Sponges*, published in 1921, writes: 'The sponge-fisheries of Crete, which are very important, are carried on entirely by fishermen from other Greek islands, who arrive in the spring and return in the autumn to their native places with their catches.' If this was true in 1921, it was probably true thirty years earlier.

According to my theory the sponge-fishers then took the Treasure back to their native island of Aegina, where George Brown deposited it in a fake burial in a Mycenaean tomb which he had previously discovered in his vineyard on Windmill Hill.

The reason for this elaborate hoax would be to divert attention from the real source of the Treasure in Crete because (a) Crete was still under Turkish control, and the Turks were not kind to tomb-robbers; (b) the find-spot in Crete was still a potential source of supply, and must be protected; (c) it was essential for George Brown to acquire some legal title to the Treasure.

Where was this Cretan find-spot? A strong candidate was a royal tomb belonging to the ancient palace at Mallia on the north-east coast of Crete (10). Known locally as Chrysolakkos (or the 'gold-hole'), it was said to have been extensively robbed of gold objects about the 1880s. The gold was believed to have been melted down – a common practice amongst tomb-robbers for obvious reasons – but of this there was no proof. The tomb was subsequently excavated scientifically by French archaeologists, and the few gleanings left by the looters did in fact provide almost the only known parallels to the more unusual aspects of the Treasure. To judge by the pottery, the tomb was used repeatedly by the royalty and nobility of Mallia between 1900 and 1600 BC. I would date the few surviving pieces of gold to the end of this period, between 1700 and 1600 BC because (in accordance with the custom in Crete at that time) any gold from earlier burials would have been removed by the mourners at subsequent interments. Once the flesh had left their bones the dead were evidently considered to be of no importance, to be robbed with impunity.

These theories were aired in a couple of lectures which I gave in London in 1957. They were subsequently published in the *Bulletin of the Institute of Classical Studies* of London University and in the *Annual of the British School at Athens* for that year.

I still hold to my views as to the date and place of manufacture of the Treasure: the reasons for these views are given in the next Chapter. As for my theory of its finding-place, I will return to it later in the book.

CHAPTER THREE

Description of the Treasure

The time has now come to give a brief description of the Treasure, in the light of my research of 1956–7, as modified (very slightly) by a few subsequent reconsiderations, and amplified by a little additional evidence.

For those who require more detailed factual information a fuller catalogue will be found in the Appendix. To those even more curious the original article in the *Annual of the British School at Athens* for 1957 may be of interest.

The most important object in the Treasure is no. 1 (**11**). It shows a Cretan god standing in a field of lotus-flowers; the lotus was a kind of water-lily which was very popular in Egyptian art. In either hand he holds a goose by the neck, and behind are two mysterious objects which probably represent sacred bull's horns or (less probably) composite bows.

The god wears a tall feather-head-dress, large circular earrings, bracelets on his wrists and upper arms, a tightly fitting tunic, shorts, and a tight belt with an embroidered tassel. We know he is a Cretan god of the Minoan period from his dress: it is one of the three regular Cretan male fashions, the other two being a loin-cloth and a kilt. We may assume from the objects with him that he is a nature-god; but we do not know his name. This god is known to archaeologists as the Master of Animals, the uncommon (but well authenticated) male version of the universal Minoan Mistress of Animals, who was to become Artemis to the later Greeks.

Five gold discs, decorated with raised dots, hang from the bottom of this ornament. They may perhaps represent the sun.

What was the purpose of this intriguing gold pendant? It was evidently made to hang from a cord or a wire; or most probably from a long dress-pin, because that is the purpose of the only similar object we know – a gold relief of a Cretan goddess which was found attached to a silver pin in a royal grave at Mycenae of the sixteenth century BC (**12**).

A date slightly earlier than the Mycenae pin is suggested by three pieces of gold jewellery of about 1700–1600 BC from the royal tomb at Mallia in North Crete (see above, p. 21), which resemble parts of our pendant. This was the time when the Royal Palaces in Crete, whose ruins are standing today, had just been built, and Crete was at its most prosperous: a period when we might expect to find jewellery of the highest quality.

One resemblance is provided by a gold lotus-flower (**13**) which is very like one of the three lotuses by the god's feet. The second is the set of pendant discs on the famous bee-jewel from Mallia, which is one of the glories of the Archaeological Museum at Heraklion and is so well-known as to have become almost the trademark of Crete (**14**). The third is a figure of a leaf (**15**) which resembles the pendant discs of our piece in the dotted decoration and in its suspension-loop.

11 Gold pendant from the Treasure: the Master of Animals. It may come from a dress-pin.

12 Silver dress-pin with a gold pendant relief of a Cretan goddess. From the Third Shaft Grave at Mycenae. The pendant in illus. 11 may have come from a similar pin.

13 Gold pendant in the form of a lotus flower; from the Chrysolakkos tomb at Mallia.

14 Two bees (or less probably wasps or hornets), posed heraldically across a honeycomb, make a decorative gold pendant. From the Chrysolakkos tomb at Mallia.

The Cretan artist, working in the seventeenth century BC, is clearly acquainted with Egyptian tomb wall-paintings of the owner hunting wild birds in a marsh from a reed-boat (16) – it was a very popular scene for over two thousand years. But he has completely altered this picture to suit his ideas, and has converted an Egyptian nobleman into a Cretan god.

We have here, then, in all probability an ornament from a dress-pin in the form of a nature-god, made in Crete between 1700 and 1600 BC.

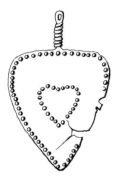

15 *Left* Gold pendant in the shape of a leaf. From the Chrysolakkos tomb at Mallia.

16 Wall-painting from an Egyptian tomb showing the owner wild-fowling in the marshes. Possibly the inspiration for the pendant, illus. 11.

No. 2 is composed of two pairs of gold earrings (**17, 64, 65**). Within a hoop in the form of a double-headed snake are a pair of greyhounds, face to face; below them are a pair of monkeys, back to back. From the circumference hang fourteen pendants on gold chains, seven in the form of owls (probably the Little Owl) and seven in the form of discs. Cornelian beads are threaded on gold wires in various places to add a contrasting note of red.

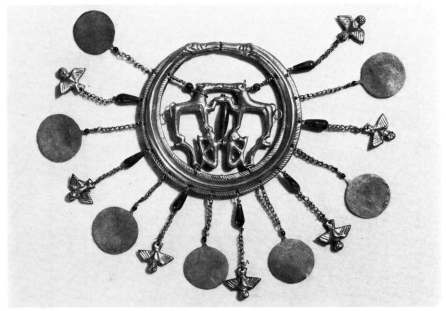

17 A gold earring from the Treasure. A double-headed snake encloses two hounds face-to-face and two monkeys back-to-back. Gold discs and owl-figures hang by chains from the snake.

A small gold bird like the owls, but not identical with them, was found in the royal tomb at Mallia in Crete mentioned above (**18**). So we may see these earrings also as Cretan of the seventeenth century BC.

No other earrings at all like these are known, but it is hard to see what else they could be; and in a recently discovered fresco from Thera of the sixteenth century BC a lady wears what could be a simplified version of them (**19**).

18 A small bird-pendant from the Chrysolakkos tomb at Mallia, recalling the owls of illus. **17**.

The subject matter is also very puzzling, but monkeys like these, either singly or in pairs, are known in Cretan art of about this period (**20**). The overall design may well have been inspired by some piece of Egyptian jewellery such as a gold pectoral (**21**). Here, again, the Cretan craftsman can be seen to have adapted a foreign subject to his own purposes, and in doing so to have completely changed its character.

19 A lady in a fresco from Thera wears an earring which looks like a simplified version of illus. 17.

20 A monkey on a seal-impression from Phaestos looks very like the monkeys of illus. 17.

21 An Egyptian gold pectoral of about 1850 BC may have inspired illus. 17.

No. 3 is composed of a curved plate of gold with a human head in profile looking out from either end (**22**). The eyes and eyebrows were originally inlaid with a blue substance, probably lapis lazuli, which would have added a discreet touch of a contrasting colour to stand out against the gold.

This type of head, with the hair combed back and ending in curls, is perhaps more typical of a sphinx than a human in Cretan art. A good example of a sphinx with a head like these is to be found on a Cretan seal of about 1750 BC (**23**). The actual features, however, are closer to a seal-impression of about 1700 BC (**24**).

The rings on the tops of the heads are for a cord or chain and show that this ornament was worn round the neck. The discs which hang from it associate it with the nature-god, no. 1; and so we may regard this too as Cretan work of the seventeenth century BC.

22 A gold pectoral from the Treasure. It terminates in two human heads in profile. The typical 'Greek profile' is anticipated by about a thousand years.

23 *Left* A Cretan seal with an impression of a sphinx might suggest that the heads of illus. **22** could also be sphinx-heads.

24 *Below* A Cretan seal-impression of a male head has a similar profile to illus. **22**.

No. 4, another gold ornament (**25**), is rather more of a problem piece; it is probably an earring. The principal element is a lion's head rising from a collar decorated with filigree spirals. Below the collar a hollow basket-like receptacle hangs by means of a gold pin. Some object of a perishable nature (ivory or amber?) was once threaded on the pin but is now lost. Two pendants representing birds (probably ducks) and two representing eggs hang by chains from the collar; three more birds hang in the same way from the receptacle.

The birds associate this mysterious object with the earrings, no. 2. It is not easy to guess the appearance of the missing element. Probably the complete object was a model of a ceremonial axe-head, like the one from the Palace at Mallia (**26**), made about 1700 BC.

25 An earring (?) from the Treasure. Five figures of ducks, and two of eggs, hang from a complicated ornament incorporating a lion's head.

26 A ceremonial stone axe-head from the Palace at Mallia, with a lion's head butt, has something in common with illus. 25.

No. 5 is a tantalizing fragment from another piece of gold jewellery (**27**) which may well have been like no. 2 or perhaps no. 4. All that survives are two figures of owls hanging by chains from a gold-capped cornelian bead. This fragment, and a few others, suggest that the Treasure, as we have it, is not complete.

27 A small gold pendant with owls, from the Treasure. Possibly from a composite ornament like illus. 17.

No. 6 consists of fifty-four identical gold discs (**28**), pierced for attachment to the dress or the shroud which a dead lady was wearing. They are decorated by means of impressed dots with a rosette surrounded by eight connected spirals. There are parallels in details with objects from royal burials at Mycenae of the sixteenth century BC (**29**). This, then could be the date of these discs.

28 A few of the 54 gold discs from the Treasure which probably decorated the burial-shroud of a Cretan lady.

29 A gold diadem from the Fourth Shaft Grave at Mycenae.

The two diadems, no. 7 (**30**) are simpler versions of the many embossed diadems found in royal burials at Mycenae dated between 1700 and 1500 BC. They were worn by the owner (who could be male or female) probably in life as in death, round the brow, fastened by a cord passing through the looped ends.

A third diadem, no. 8, is decorated by means of raised dots with two lines of returning spirals (**30**). Decoration with raised dots is an early feature, and is seldom found after 1600 BC. But I cannot find sure evidence for this particular pattern much before that date. So perhaps we should date this diadem about 1600 BC.

No. 9 consists of a number of thin gold bands. Such bands, for sewing on (women's?) clothing, were made in Crete between 2500 and 1600 BC, but no later; and we cannot date these bands any closer than that.

No. 10 is a massive gold bracelet without decoration (**31**). It is impossible to date such an object, but it is interesting to note its resemblance in a general sort of way to Egyptian bracelets of about 1450 BC.

31 A chunky gold bracelet from the Treasure.

No. 11 consists of two necklaces of beads in the shape of palm-leaves (**32**). Exactly similar beads were found in a royal burial at Mycenae of the sixteenth century BC, and this will be the date of our beads.

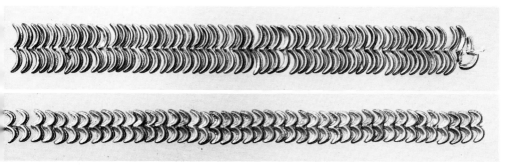

32 Two necklaces of interlocking palm-leaf beads, from the Treasure.
30 *Left* Three gold diadems, two plain and one fancy, from the Treasure.

No. 12 consists of eleven beads in the form of a right hand holding a woman's breast (33). Three are of cornelian; three of lapis lazuli (a semi-precious stone of an intense blue colour); and five of gold. No beads of this form are recorded elsewhere, but a Cretan origin of the seventeenth or sixteenth century BC might be deduced from the use of lapis lazuli also in the rings nos. 12–16, and possibly in no. 3. The motif of a woman pressing her naked breasts had a long history in Western Asia, where it was associated with fertility goddesses under various names. It occasionally strayed into the Aegean, and we find a good example in a figurine-vase from Mochlos in East Crete of 2200–2000 BC (34). More Asiatic influence can be seen in the association of gold, cornelian and lapis lazuli in beads of the same kind, a conjunction which is particularly common in the Royal Graves at Ur of about 2700 BC. Some religious symbolism was probably intended.

33 Identical beads of gold, cornelian and lapis lazuli in the shape of a hand holding a woman's breast. From the Treasure.

34 Figurine-vase from Mochlos in Crete showing a mother-goddess holding her breasts in a manner recalling illus. 33.

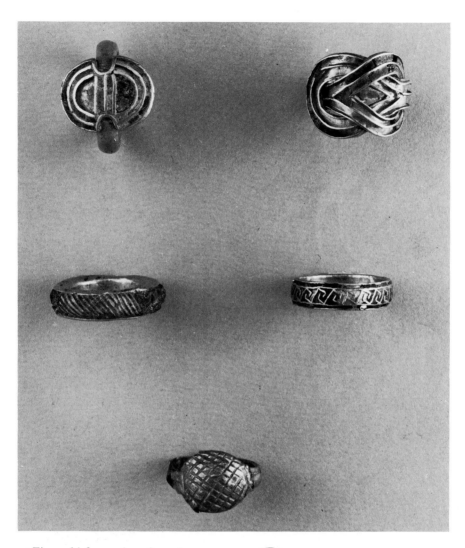

35 Five gold finger-rings from the Treasure. The four top ones are inlaid with lapis lazuli. The bottom one is very flimsy and must have covered a core of some other material, such as bronze or glass.

36 A cup from Mochlos in Crete decorated with a meander-pattern like one of the rings in illus. 35.

Nos. 13–16 are gold finger-rings, inlaid with lapis lazuli (**35**). In the outer surface of no. 13 the lapis lazuli serves as a background for an oblique meander pattern in gold. A not dissimilar ring, inlaid with the same material, comes (rather surprisingly) from a Royal Tomb at Ur of about 2500 BC. In Greek lands the earliest recorded inlaid ring comes from a Cretan tomb of the mid-sixteenth century BC. The seventeenth century BC, is, however, suggested for this ring by the pattern, which is paralleled on a handled vase from Mochlos in East Crete of that date (**36**).

In no. 14 the outer surface is inlaid with two parallel rows of lapis lazuli; the bezel is in the form of a reef-knot, also of gold, inlaid with two rows of lapis lazuli. In Greek art the reef-knot was not common before Hellenistic times, but this is not a Hellenistic ring. In Egypt, however, it is common in jewellery of the XIIth Dynasty in the nineteenth century BC. On technical grounds this ring must be contemporary with no. 13, and so should probably be dated in the seventeenth or sixteenth century BC.

No. 15 is composed of a solid gold hoop, flat inside and rounded outside, with an oval bezel set at right-angles to it. The bezel has two semi-circular indentations, and is inlaid, like nos. 13 and 14, with lapis lazuli. At first sight the bezel would be taken to represent the so-called Boeotian shield of the eighth century BC and later. This has in fact been the opinion of those advocating a late date for the Treasure. If, however, we treat the ring as a Minoan ring and 'read' it not vertically but horizontally, we find a perfectly normal Minoan ceremonial double-axe such as the axe reproduced on a vase of the sixteenth century BC (**37**).

37 A representation of a double-axe on a Cretan vase of 1600–1500 BC which explains the subject-matter of one of the rings in illus. 35.

No. 16 is in the form of a thin plate, with both edges turned outwards. The groove so formed is filled with lapis lazuli, fluted diagonally. No exact parallels are known, but it is clear from the technique and from the materials that it is contemporary with nos. 13–15.

We have then in nos. 13–16 a self-contained group, to be dated in all probability in the seventeenth or sixteenth century BC.

No. 17 consists of the bezel and part of the hoop of a ring of thin gold foil. The bezel is a convex oval, decorated with cross-hatched lines; the hoop is grooved down the middle. Since the gold is much too flimsy to have existed by itself, it must have been wrapped round a core of some other material now perished, such as wood, ivory, or glass. A Cretan origin, of about 1700–1600 BC is probable if we go by what little comparative evidence there is.

The five plain gold hoops, no. 18 (**38**), could have been made at any time, and for a number of purposes. If, however, they are (like so much of the Treasure) Cretan of the seventeenth or sixteenth century BC then we should probably see them as earrings worn linked together, and can be compared with a seventeenth-century Cretan face-bead (**39**).

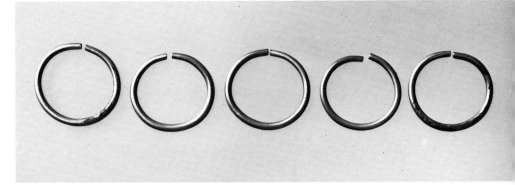

38 Five plain gold rings from the Treasure, possibly linked together and worn as earrings.

39 A face bead from the Jewel Fresco at Knossos. Note the earrings, like illus. 38.

All the remaining beads and pendants of the Treasure have been grouped together in nos. 19 to 22. So far as 19 and 21 are concerned, the arrangement is purely arbitrary, and has been made purely for convenience of display.

In the necklace no. 19 three sorts of gold beads have been grouped together (**40a**). The collared beads with circular depressions are, as far as I know, unique. The spherical and biconical beads are, on the contrary, so common in ancient jewellery as to be virtually undatable. The egg-shaped pendants on chains, however, remind us of the 'eggs' on the earring no. 4, with which they are probably contemporary.

40 *Opposite* Three necklaces from the Treasure. The beads are of gold, green jasper, cornelian and amethyst. The arrangement is arbitrary.

The necklace no. 20 consists of eighty gold melon-shaped beads (**40b**), which are so common as to be undatable; and fifteen gold-capped beads of green jasper, which are (as far as I know) unique, and so equally undatable.

In no. 21 have been collected all the beads from the Treasure in cornelian and amethyst (**40c**). Both stones are varieties of quartz, coloured reddish-brown and purple respectively, and were especially popular with Cretan seal-engravers.

The spherical cornelians and the one oval cornelian are so common as to be undatable. The cornelian barrel-shaped and cylindrical beads are less common, and remind us so strongly of the beads attached to the earrings, no. 2, that they probably come from similar earrings.

The three amethyst beads are pierced in three places to serve as spacing beads in a three-stringed necklace. An identical bead was found in a royal burial at Knossos of the sixteenth century BC; so we can date these beads accordingly.

No. 22 is a flanged disc-bead of rock-crystal, perforated diametrically (**41**). The purpose of the flange is to take a cord for the attachment of a pendant. Beads of this shape are very rare but several were found in a tomb at Mochlos in Crete together with other beads which appear to date between 1650 and 1550 BC.

41 Flanged bead of rock-crystal, from the Treasure.

The last item of the Treasure is a magnificent gold cup, no. 23, with a concave rim, decorated in relief with a rosette at the bottom and with spirals running round the bowl (**42, 43**). The handle is now missing, but was originally attached with rivets. In metal, only one close parallel is known (unprovenanced), but for certain features we may compare a silver cup from a house at Knossos (**44**) and a gold goblet from a royal burial at Mycenae (**45**), both dated 1600 to 1500 BC. A pottery vase from Melos of the same date (**46**) is closer to the shape of our gold cup.

42, 43 Gold cup, from the Treasure. The handle is missing; it was originally attached with three rivets.

44 A silver cup from Knossos. A simplified version of illus. 42.

It would thus appear that those elements of the Treasure which can be dated were made either in the seventeenth or the sixteenth century BC. Most were certainly made in Crete. Some could perhaps have been made in the Mycenaean world; but it would be permissible, I think, to regard the Treasure as entirely Cretan, since the only similar objects to occur in graves at Mycenae are just the sort of things which could well have been imported from Crete.

It is not clear how many personal sets of jewellery are represented here. Nor do we know whether the wearers were male or female, for our knowledge of Cretan customs tells us that jewellery was worn by both sexes. But I suspect that most of the Aegina jewellery was worn, in death as in life, by the womenfolk.

How would these people have looked? For a Cretan man there is no better example than the Nature God, our no. 1 (11), with his fancy head-dress, his earrings and his multiple bracelets. We might also imagine him with strings of beads round his neck and wrists. Women of our period are best known from statuettes of bronze or faience (47) and from the newly-discovered frescoes from the island of Thera.

It will be seen at a glance how utterly different was the appearance of these people from that of the classical Greeks, whom we know so well from sculptures and vase-paintings: nearer in some respects to the Orient of those days, in others to our own day.

47 *Overleaf* One of the faience Snake Goddesses from Knossos. Cretan ladies must have looked, and dressed, very much like this.

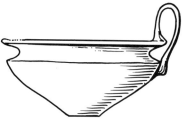

45 A gold goblet from the Fifth Shaft Grave at Mycenae. The bowl is not unlike the gold cup, illus. 42.

46 A pottery cup from Melos, of the same shape as illus. 42.

CHAPTER FOUR

Doubts and Reappraisals, 1959–1977

Such, then, is the Aegina Treasure, rich, beautiful and still mysterious. And such were my views in 1957.

So far as the place and date of manufacture are concerned, I have had no reason to change my mind. But my ingenious theory as to the find-spot of the Treasure was not to stand the test of time.

In April 1959, through the good offices of a friend, Mrs Eugenia Papaleonardou, whose husband had a family house at Aegina, I had the opportunity to meet George Brown, son of the George Brown who had sold the Treasure to the British Museum. He told me that his father had found it in a chamber-tomb with a sloping entrance-passage on his land on Windmill Hill. A workman accidentally broke through the roof of the chamber when planting vines, and in it was the Treasure, which included a gold doll. The position was shown to me, near a hexagonal-shaped house; but the tomb, I was told, had been filled in and the ground levelled off. He said that his father had had much trouble with the authorities over this business.

This account carried so much conviction that I began at once to suspect that my theory of a Cretan find-spot was just too clever to be true. The gold doll, however, was a new development which I could not understand. It was to crop up again.

And so, disappointed though still not entirely convinced, I suspended judgement and waited for further evidence to come to light. I waited for seventeen years without avail, but in 1976 things started to happen again. In July of that year I received an unexpected visit at the Greek and Roman Department of the British Museum from an American lawyer by the name of Michel Emmanuel, and his wife. They wished to see certain pieces from the Aegina Treasure which had been temporarily withdrawn from exhibition during building works.

Whilst we were examining these pieces together in my study, Mr Emmanuel remarked that his grandfather had been employed by the firm of Cresswell Brothers in Aegina at the time of the discovery. On hearing of my interest, he promised to let me have the story as handed down in his family. This, I thought, could well be the break-through for which I had been waiting.

Mr Emmanuel was as good as his word, and a week later I received a letter so interesting that I reproduce it almost in full, omitting only irrelevancies.

'1. *Cresswell Bros of London*. During the middle and last half of the 19th century, the sponge industry in Greece became an important part of the economy due largely to the development of the compressed air diving suit. Greek sponge divers from Aegina and a number of other islands ranged the Mediterranean in search of commercial sponges. One of the marketing centers for the sponges was Aegina where Cresswell Bros, a London firm, maintained an office and sponge packing house. Their business included the purchase of sponges as well as the sale of diving equipment and other items of chandlery. Their agent and manager was George Brown, an Englishman whose prestige in Aegina and Athens was substantial. In the late 1870's or early 1880's Brown built a three-story home on the Aegina waterfront which has since been converted into a hotel known as "Hotel Brown" (**48, 49**). Commencing in 1879 when he was 22 years of age, my grandfather, Michel Emmanuel, became Brown's assistant (**50**).

'2. *Discovery of the Treasure*. In or about 1880, while a parcel of Aegina land belonging to George Brown was being cultivated, an ancient tomb was discovered. In it was a number of artifacts, including several beautiful pieces of gold jewelry. One of the items was a gold doll. My efforts to get a better description of the gold doll have been unsuccessful. My father and three of his sisters, with whom I discussed the matter, had never seen either the treasure or the doll and could not describe the doll as to size, weight or other characteristics. They could only assure me that the treasure had existed and that the doll had gotten grandfather into a lot of trouble. After the treasure was discovered, my best information is that it was reburied by George Brown in his cellar where it remained until after his death.

'3. *Disappearance of the Gold Doll*. George Brown died in 1887 and was interred in the main cemetery in Aegina. His grave is marked by an impressive obelisk. Following her husband's death, Mrs George Brown decided to return to England. Before she boarded her ship she persuaded my grandfather, Michel Emmanuel, to help her sneak the gold doll out of Greece. During the night before her departure grandfather had two men row him out to Mrs Brown's ship where he delivered the doll to her. The ship sailed the next day but Mrs Brown never reached England. She died en route and was buried at sea. To the best of my knowledge the gold doll was never seen or heard of again. It may well have been on Mrs Brown's person when she was committed to the deep.

'4. *Epilogue*. One of the boatmen who rowed grandfather to Mrs Brown's ship later reported to the authorities that grandfather had helped smuggle out an ancient artifact. In legal proceedings which continued over a number of years, grandfather was convicted of the act. He had many friends in high places who came to his aid, including the British Ambassador to Greece who was a good friend of the Brown family. As a result, grandfather was pardoned. In the meantime George Brown, Jr (**50**) had succeeded his father as Cresswell's agent in Aegina but due to his youth and inexperience grandfather performed most of the duties of that office. In 1891 George Brown, Jr was relieved of his duties as Cresswell's agent and was succeeded by my grandfather. George Brown, Jr returned to England and one may assume that he took the rest of the Aegina Treasure with him since it was offered to the British Museum a short time thereafter. Grandfather continued to perform his duties for Cresswell Bros until 1905. At that time he left Greece with my father to recoup his fortunes in the United States. He died in Tarpon Springs, Florida, in 1913'.

48 The south harbour front at Aegina with the Hotel Brown.

49 The Hotel Brown at Aegina, formerly the town house of the Brown family.

50 The staff of Cresswell Bros., about 1890. Seated, left to right: George Brown the second; Frederic R. Cresswell, the head of the firm; Michel Emmanuel. The standing figures are Greek employees.

Here was a mine of information, some of it rather unexpected. In the first place, there were evidently not two but three generations of George Browns: the first, a very respected figure, believed by Mr Emmanuel to have found the Treasure, who died in 1887; the second, believed by me to have found it; and the third, whom I had met in 1959 (**53**). Secondly, the re-appearance of the 'gold doll' surprised me, as I had previously been inclined to doubt its existence. And thirdly, a date as early as 1880 or so for the discovery of the Treasure came as another surprise, as I could not see the sense of keeping anything so 'hot' on the premises for over ten years.

51 The Temple of Apollo and the Hexagonal House from the port.

52 The Temple of Apollo and the Hexagonal House from the north-west.

53 George Brown the third, with Mrs Papaleonardou, photographed at Aegina in 1959.

Yet in spite of these problems, Mr Emmanuel's story had basically the ring of truth, and I was now convinced at last that George Brown really had found the Treasure in a tomb in his Windmill Hill vineyard.

Later that year another piece of the jigsaw puzzle fell into place. I happened to see, for the first time a posthumous second edition (in Greek) of Welter's *Aegina*, written about 1950 but not published till 1962, eight years after his death. It contained an account of the discovery of the Treasure, considerably more circumstantial than in his first edition. Possibly he no longer saw the need for reticence, and could now speak more freely.

After mentioning the Mycenaean graves on the slope of Windmill Hill facing Kolonna (i.e. the West slope), Welter goes on: 'The Brown treasure bought in 1891 by the British Museum, comprising 24 pieces of gold jewellery and plate, was found while digging for the foundations of the octagonal tower of the half-built Brown (now D. Petritis) house, in a chamber-tomb which had been robbed in antiquity before the treasure had been hidden in it. The treasure was made up of the contents of various other robbed tombs.'

Here at last was a little firm ground in the midst of the shifting sands and here (as I understood it) was the counter-suggestion by Welter that the Treasure did after all come from an Aeginetan cemetery.

Clearly another visit to Aegina was indicated; and I was fortunate enough to make it in May 1977 in the company of Mr and Mrs Emmanuel.

We saw the Brown-Petritis house (which incidentally was not octagonal but hexagonal, but no matter) and found it to be somewhat to the north of the tombs excavated by Keramopoullos and Welter, on the western slope of Windmill Hill, facing the Temple (51, 52). It had been bought from the Brown family by Mr D. Petritis and was now occupied by his son, General Constantine Petritis. Mr Emmanuel introduced me to his cousin, Mrs Stella Xeflouda, an old resident in Aegina. She confirmed the essentials of the story of the discovery as told to me by the third George Brown and as recorded by Welter in the 1962 book. She added that the hexagonal house was originally a windmill; George Brown (the second) started to convert it, but it was not finished till after it had been bought by Petritis.

We also met Mr Demetrios Panges who had formerly been the guardian of the Aegina Museum for thirty years. He had been retired for a long time, being 78 years old. His information, he said, came from Mr A. Pelekanos, the first director of the Museum from its foundation in 1898.

Mr Panges's memory was hazy, but he was certain that the Treasure and the gold doll were entirely separate. His story was that the doll was found by George Brown's men near the prison (in the south part of the town); was taken to Brown's town house (now the Hotel Brown); and ended up in the British Museum. (This last is not true, and must result from a confusion with the Treasure.) He pointed out a stone sarcophagus in the Aegina Museum, about two feet long, which he said, according to Pelekanos, had once contained the gold doll. The sarcophagus was (I think) Mycenaean, and made for a child. If this story is true, the 'gold doll' must also have been Mycenaean. Could it have been a 'gold suit' for a child, like the one found by Schliemann in the Third Shaft Grave at Mycenae? Or was Panges's memory at fault and it was not Mycenaean at all, but a gilt bronze statue of Greek or Roman date? We will probably never know, but I think we must admit that the 'gold doll' did probably exist in some form.

CHAPTER FIVE

What really happened?

It should now be possible to attempt some sort of a reconstruction of the events which led to the acquisition of the Aegina Treasure by the British Museum in 1892. In this attempt every effort has been made to take into account all the relevant information, and to reconcile conflicting pieces of evidence; but it must be admitted that any consecutive story is at best a probability and not a certainty.

1 The Gold Doll

About 1880, when George Brown the first was agent and manager in Aegina of Cresswell Brothers, a London firm of sponge-merchants, his men found a 'gold doll' in a tomb on the outskirts of the town of Aegina, perhaps to the south. The doll was possibly found in a stone coffin of a type used in the Mycenaean period for the burial of children. In that case the doll would itself have been Mycenaean and may have resembled a 'gold suit' found by Schliemann in a royal child's burial at Mycenae of the sixteenth century BC.

The doll was taken to Brown's town house on the Aegina waterfront (now the Hotel Brown), where it was kept concealed in a cellar. On Brown's death in 1887 his widow left for England, taking the doll with her. She unfortunately died on the voyage, and the doll was heard of no more; it was perhaps buried with her at sea. It subsequently became something of a legend, and its story took precedence over that of the Treasure, which was as good as forgotten.

If this version of the story is true, then the discovery of the doll and the discovery of the Treasure are two entirely separate events.

2 The Treasure

At some time between 1887 and 1890, George Brown the second, who had in 1887 succeeded his father as agent of Cresswell Brothers, was planting vines on his property on Windmill Hill, just north of Aegina town and east of Cape Kolonna, which happened to be on the site of an ancient cemetery.

Very close to a disused windmill on the western slope of the hill, facing the temple, a workman accidentally broke through the roof of the rectangular burial chamber of a Mycenaean tomb. There was evidence that the tomb had previously been entered and robbed, but in one corner of the chamber was found, roughly buried, a mass of gold objects and a number of coloured stone beads. Scattered about the tomb were also some Mycenaean vases, at least six in number, ranging in date between 1350 and 1150 BC.

In order to 'conceal his digging' (evidence of Harland) Brown went through the motions of converting the windmill into a dwelling-house. The house was still unfinished in 1904, as Keramopoullos refers casually to 'Brown's half-finished tower'. In fact, the conversion was not completed till many years later, when the property was bought by Mr D. Petritis.

The Treasure was hurriedly removed from the tomb and concealed. It was kept intact except for a few beads, which were given as keepsakes to the family governess, Miss Sinclair.

In 1891 George Brown the second relinquished his duties as Cresswell's agent and returned to England, taking with him the gold treasure, which he offered to the British Museum for £6000 and sold in the following year for £4000. In spite of attempts at secrecy the general situation of the find-spot soon leaked out, and the Treasure was henceforth known as the Aegina Treasure. The Greek authorities tried hard to locate the tomb and to elicit the truth from the Brown family, but all to no avail; and eventually the matter was allowed to rest.

Can we go further, and explain how this Treasure, made in Crete between 1700 and 1500 BC, found its way into a Mycenaean tomb near the town of Aegina which was not occupied (or indeed built) before 1350 BC?

Clearly, as Welter saw long ago, the Treasure, as found, was a robbers' cache. He believed that it was loot from a tomb-robbery and I think we may accept this view, as (with certain exceptions) objects of this value seldom survive from antiquity except when buried with the dead. But when and where did the ancient robbery take place?

First, when? It would in any case be after the last legitimate occupation of the Mycenaean tomb used as a cache by the robbers; that is to say, after 1150 BC. My own guess is that it would have been not long after this date, before the existence of the tombs involved (the tomb or tombs robbed and the Mycenaean tomb) had been forgotten. The eleventh or tenth century BC would be suitable on this and on other grounds, for the Bronze Age was now at an end, newcomers had occupied many parts of Greece, and law and order had for the time being ceased to exist.

Secondly, where? Welter had suggested in 1938 that the Treasure may have come ultimately from outside Aegina, but gave no reason for this surprising remark. In the 1962 edition of *Aigina* the suggestion is dropped, and we may suppose that he no longer believed in it. It is of course theoretically possible for ancient tomb-robbers to have looted a cemetery on Crete and to have taken the loot to Aegina, but it does not seem likely. There is in fact no valid reason why the Treasure should not have been stolen from one or more tombs belonging to the Middle and Late Bronze Age settlement on Cape Kolonna. As it happens, no tombs of 1700 to 1500 BC belonging to this settlement have yet been found (perhaps they are under the modern town) and we are now unlikely to find them or to see any comparable goldwork. We do know, however, that the settlement was in close touch with Crete about this time, for they were importing a certain amount of fine Minoan pottery in the nineteenth and eighteenth centuries BC, which stands out in marked contrast to the bulk of the pottery, the 'Matt-painted' ware typical of mainland Greece.

It remains to speculate whether Aegina at this date contained a Cretan element in its population as owners of the Treasure or whether the local inhabitants were rich enough to import Cretan goldwork of this quality. I do not think we are dealing with an outpost of a Minoan Empire, for this is essentially a Greek, not a Cretan, city with its massive fortification walls and its predominantly Matt-painted pottery.

I think there is overwhelming evidence for a Cretan element in the population at the time when the Treasure was in use. In 1937, Welter, describing his recent excavations at Kolonna, had deduced the presence of Cretan potters in the settlement between 1900 and 1700 BC. He says: 'Middle Minoan II (1900–1700 B.C.) is represented by imported Cretan Kamares Ware (54). At the same time this pottery was imitated in Aegina. This could scarcely have been done by local potters (for technical reasons) but by Cretans who had

54 Cretan pottery fragments in the Kamares Style of 1900–1700 BC. Found in the ruins of the prehistoric city at Aegina.

settled in Aegina.' He next mentions his discovery at Kolonna of a potter's-wheel disc of Cretan clay, identical with many examples excavated on a number of Cretan sites, which, he says, clinches the existence of Cretan potters on Aegina at this time. We could go further, and deduce that Cretan potters could only have worked for Cretan customers, for we know that the local Aeginetans made and used a very different type of pottery (Matt-painted Ware). A further piece of evidence is contributed by a short inscription in the Cretan 'Linear A' script which Welter also found at the Kolonna site.

There is, moreover, evidence for a Cretan presence at an early period on the other side of the island. Pausanias, a Greek travel-writer of the second century

AD, says that the temple on the north-east coast was dedicated to Aphaia, a goddess known in Crete as Diktynna or Britomartis. The temple Pausanias saw had been built as late as the fifth century BC, but the sanctuary was certainly in existence in the Late Bronze Age, and a Cretan goddess implies (in the first instance) Cretan worshippers. In any event, the presence on Aegina of Cretan jewellery and gold plate of such high quality (however it got there) would suggest that this island was even more important in the period in question than is usually believed. I do not believe that the Treasure is too rich to have been the property of one or more well-to-do Cretan families on Aegina. In fact, fine as it is, the quality is not as high as contemporary jewellery from the palatial centres of Knossos and Mallia (cf. 14); for example, there is no granulation and practically no filigree.

This is not the only instance of the discovery in recent times of an ancient tomb-robbers' cache on a Mycenaean site. One was found in an empty shaft-grave on the Acropolis at Mycenae; another in the ruins of a Late Mycenaean house at Tiryns. But why, in these cases, did the robbers not return to collect their loot? We can only guess that they were prevented; killed in battle perhaps, or caught robbing another tomb and dealt with according to the rough justice of the time.

Perhaps we can fill in the details from what we know about tomb-robbery in ancient Egypt, especially from the accounts of the trials of tomb-robbers recorded in papyri of the Twentieth Dynasty. Cyril Aldred quotes a contemporary account of the arrest and confession in 1124 BC of a certain Amun-pnufer; he had robbed the tomb of a Pharaoh of the Seventeenth Dynasty, who had lived over four centuries earlier.

'We found the noble mummy of the sacred king', he said. 'Numerous golden amulets and ornaments were upon his breast and a golden mask was over his face. The noble mummy of this king was entirely bedecked with gold and his coffins were embellished with gold and silver, both inside and out, and inlaid with precious stones. We collected the gold together with the amulets and jewels that were about him and the metal that was on his coffins. We found the queen in the same state and retrieved all that we found upon her. Then we set fire to their coffins. We took the furnishings that we found with them comprising objects of gold, silver and bronze and divided the spoils amongst us . . .'

So, we may imagine, might our tomb-robber or robbers have behaved at much the same time. There are signs that the Aegina Treasure is in fact part of a larger haul. Perhaps the loot had already been divided, and each of the robbers had gone off with his share, to be melted down as soon as possible. Our robber would have buried his portion in a Mycenaean chamber-tomb he had previously found. But then, for reasons at which we can only guess, he was prevented from coming back for his ill-gotten gains, and his Treasure remained hidden in the tomb until Brown's men stumbled on it some three thousand years later.

CHAPTER SIX

The Cretan Goldsmith

How did the Cretans, nearly four thousand years ago, achieve such mastery over their material when the tools and techniques at their command can only have been of the simplest? Their manual dexterity must evidently have more than made up for the technical limitations under which they worked.

To start at the beginning, the goldsmith would receive his gold in the form of bars, or ingots. We do not know where the gold originated; there was certainly none in Crete and probably none in Mycenaean Greece. Of the areas with which the Cretans were in touch, Egypt was rich in this respect, and could well have supplied it. Another likely source is North Syria, near the mouth of the river Orontes, where the Melas valley is known to have been rich in alluvial gold.

What could the Cretans have offered in exchange? We know that the Egyptians imported fine Cretan pottery at this date as it has been found in Egypt and was also represented on wall-paintings in tombs, and we may guess that they also imported olive-oil, timber and wool from the same source, to make good their own deficiencies. So far as Syria is concerned, we have documentary evidence on cuneiform tablets from Mari on the Middle Euphrates that they were importing vases, textiles and weapons from Crete at just about the time that the Treasure was being made.

The gold used in antiquity was almost pure, with only a few natural impurities remaining; it would be about 23 carat on modern reckoning. Such gold is extremely soft (no harder than lead) and would today be considered too soft for everyday use. But it had two advantages: it was easy to work, and it was a very good colour.

There are three basic elements of which all ancient goldwork was formed: sheet metal, wire, and cast metal. All occur in the Treasure, but the third very rarely.

1 Sheet Gold

This is made by setting an ingot on an anvil and beating it repeatedly with a pebble or a round-faced hammer. When the metal becomes hard and brittle, as it soon will, it is annealed by bringing it up to red heat in a charcoal fire and letting it cool. When the metal is thin enough, any hammer-marks are removed with a burnishing-tool and the surface is polished with an abrasive powder.

The strips, no. 9, were left in this condition, but as a rule the gold was shaped or embellished in some way. For example, the cup, no. 23, was *raised* from a disc of sheet gold by hammering it over a convex *stake*. The decoration was then applied freehand and a handle riveted on.

Most of the jewellery of the Treasure was made from embossed sheet-gold. It is certain in some cases (for example the earrings, no. 2) and probable in all, that some system of mass-production was employed to shape the gold. Several methods are possible (working into a mould; working over a model; stamping; or striking like a coin), but experiments in the Research Laboratory of the British Museum on one of the owls of no. 2 have suggested that they were worked into a mould, and this is possibly true of all the embossed work in the Treasure. The moulds would have been made of bronze, stone, or wood.

2 Wire

This was made by taking a narrow strip of metal, of square section, and twisting it until it looked like a stick of barley-sugar. It was then rolled between pieces of hard wood until it was round and quite smooth. The *drawplate*, which is used to make wire today, was not invented till much later.

Wire was used in the Treasure principally for making ornamental chains. These are not the simple chains we know and use today, but are of a more elaborate kind, known as loop-in-loop chains. To make such a chain, the first link is made oval in shape; the ends are soldered together; and it is bent in half. The next link, of the same shape, is threaded through the looped ends of the first, and bent in half (**55, 56**). This process is continued until the chain is complete, and it makes a very handsome chain indeed.

55 Drawing to illustrate the method of manufacture of a loop-in-loop chain.

56 A micro-photo of a loop-in-loop chain from the Treasure, which shows how the wire was made and how the link was soldered.

3 Casting

This was seldom employed for goldwork, as it was extravagant of metal, but was used to make the hoop of the ring, no. 15, and, probably, the bracelet, no. 10. A steatite mould from Cyprus, in the British Museum (**57**), was used for casting the hoop of a Mycenaean ring, and that is how no. 15 would have been made.

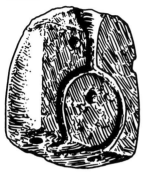

57 A steatite mould for casting a gold ring.

Most ancient jewellery was made in several pieces, which were subsequently assembled. The simplest method of joining separate elements, as in nos. 1 and 2, was to fold the edges over each other and apply pressure. A more efficient method, however, was used in the pectoral ornament, no. 3, and in completing the links of all the chains. This is known as *brazing* or *hard-soldering*. In this process, the craftsman takes a piece of the gold he is using and alloys it with silver or copper, or a mixture of the two, to lower its melting-point. This is his solder; but he also needs a flux to counteract the oxidisation which will occur when the gold is heated, and which will hold up the flow of the solder. Today we use borax, but it is unlikely that they used it in antiquity. Instead, they probably used natron, a natural combination of sodium carbonate and bicarbonate which occurs abundantly in Egypt. Both surfaces are coated with the flux, and chips of solder placed between them. The work is then wired together held by means of tongs over a charcoal fire until the correct temperature is reached, at which the solder melts and runs into the joint. The work is then removed from the fire and left to cool. When it has cooled, the joint is cleaned up by hand.

So much for the primary processes. But the excellence of ancient jewellery lay more in its superb decoration, of which several kinds are found in the Treasure.

1 Embossing

This has already been considered in connection with the making of principal forms.

2 Inlay

This was employed in the pectoral ornament, no. 3 (although the inlaid material has unfortunately perished), and in the rings nos. 13–16. The material in the rings is lapis lazuli and the pectoral was probably inlaid with the same material, if we may believe early reports. Lapis lazuli, which is also found among the beads of no. 12, and occasionally in Cretan seals, is a semi-precious stone of an intense blue colour which was mined (and still is) at Badakshan, in what is now north-east Afghanistan. It was imported from there by the Babylonians, across 1500 miles of mountain and desert country. The Syrians imported it from Babylonia and the Cretans imported it from Syria; so that by the time it got to Crete it had travelled all of 3500 miles. It must have been a very desirable material.

In this form of decoration the inlays were cut to the desired shape and cemented to the background. Frequently, as in the rings nos. 13–15, they were also secured by strips of metal, or *cloisons*, when the process is known as *cloisonné inlay*. This process is to be distinguished from a later development known as enamelling, in which the cloisons were filled with powdered glass which fused to the surface on being fired.

3 Beads
In the earrings, no. 2, beads of cornelian are threaded on thin gold wires and attached in various places. This rather clumsy technique was not used very often in antiquity.

4 Filigree
Filigree consists of fine wires soldered in patterns to a piece of jewellery. It was very popular in ancient jewellery, but is found in only one piece in the Treasure, the earring (?), no. 4. The difficulty with this sort of work was that brazing was too coarse a method of attaching the wires, and so another means had to be employed. This is known today as *colloid hard-soldering* and has the advantage that it leaves no unsightly traces of its presence, as brazing is apt to do.

This kind of solder was made by mixing a copper salt (verdigris or malachite) with gum or glue, which was used in the first instance to stick the wires to the surface. The work was then held over a charcoal fire and the heat directed on to it by means of a blowpipe. At $100°$C the copper salt changed to copper oxide; at $600°$C the gum or glue turned to carbon; at $850°$C the carbon absorbed the oxygen from the copper oxide and went off as carbon dioxide, leaving a microscopic layer of pure copper between the wires and the background; and at $890°$C the copper and the gold melted into each other and the job was done.

In a refinement of filigree, known as granulation, the wires were replaced by minute globules of gold. This beautiful method of decoration was also very popular in antiquity, and it is most surprising that there is no example of its use in the Treasure. Perhaps the reason is, as I now believe, that the Treasure was never in use in a royal court in Crete, but in the somewhat provincial centre of Aegina. The contemporary Cretan bee-jewel (**14**) and its poor relation (**61**) show what they could do in Crete at this period.

Of the stones which were incorporated in the jewellery or used separately as beads, lapis lazuli has already been mentioned. The others are all quartzes: rock-crystal, transparent and colourless; amethyst, transparent and purple; cornelian, translucent and reddish-brown; and green jasper, opaque and deep green. All would now be described as semi-precious and medium-hard (6–7 on the Mohs Scale). The Cretans probably got the rock-crystal locally in Crete and the amethyst and green jasper from Egypt. Cornelian occurs widely in nature and was probably picked up in Crete.

A modern goldsmith could not do the kind of work I have been describing without a magnifying lens, but there is no evidence for its use in antiquity. How then did the ancient craftsmen manage? For delicate work, they could have employed children, whose eyes are much more adaptable than those of adults, or they could have trained short-sighted people as goldsmiths. My own views incline to the latter alternative. After all, the great Sir Arthur Evans was a myopic, and it was his myopia which drew him to study Cretan seals, and so eventually to excavate the Palace of Minos.

Gold jewellery and plate is never found evenly distributed, like pottery, throughout cemeteries, sanctuaries and living places. In fact, because it was precious and because it could so easily be melted down by robbers, it frequently vanished without a trace from the sites of really prosperous civilizations. Consequently, the discovery of a collection like the Aegina Treasure, if we can fit it into its correct context, will considerably enlarge our knowledge of the luxury arts of its period. It does in fact give us, for the first time, some sort of a picture of the luxuries of life in a well-to-do Cretan community in the time of their greatest prosperity, that of the Second Palaces.

The Treasure clearly stands at the head of a long artistic tradition, but we know all too little about its immediate fore-runners. If we go back to the earliest period of Cretan jewellery, before the Palaces were built, we are on pretty firm ground, thanks to some very rich tombs at Mochlos in East Crete. From these we learn that Cretan jewellery of the period 2500 to 2000 BC was composed of simple beads, diadems and hair-pins of sheet gold, accompanied, rather surprisingly, by pendants on elaborate loop-in-loop gold chains. The inspiration for this jewellery reached Crete from Syria, and the Syrians had it from Babylonia.

About 2000 BC the first royal palaces were built in Crete at Knossos and elsewhere, and a very high standard of life prevailed. We know all too little about the goldsmith's art of this, the First Palace Period; but from the few scraps of gold which have been discovered it is clear that considerable technical advances had been made, including the arts of filigree, granulation, and (probably) inlay. The knowledge of these processes was due to intensified contacts with Syria. Gold and silver plate were in all likelihood plentiful, but very few examples have survived.

About 1700 BC the splendid Cretan palaces were destroyed, probably by a terrible earthquake. Nothing daunted, the Cretans set to work and built even finer palaces in their place. The Second Palace Period, from 1700 to 1450 BC, was the most brilliant of all. In many of the palatial arts we now recognize, for the first time, strong Egyptian influence supplementing the Western Asiatic influence of the previous period. To this period belongs the Aegina Treasure. If, as I believe, it was never in use in a Cretan palace, but in a comparatively provincial outpost, then we must suppose that the lords and ladies of the palaces enjoyed an even higher standard of luxury.

In addition to the Treasure, there are a few other scraps of evidence from Crete itself and elsewhere. There is of course the jewellery, already mentioned, from the cemetery belonging to the palace at Mallia, of which the bee-jewel (**14**) is the finest example. In addition, a miniature pendant in the form of a standing lion, with the mane indicated in granulation, comes from a deposit in the Palace at Knossos of about 1700 BC (**58**).

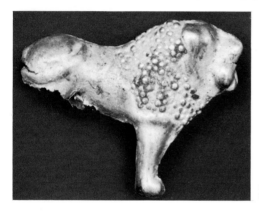

58 A gold pendant from Knossos in the form of a lion.

Then there are four pieces in the British Museum which are known to come from Crete but which have no further provenance. First, a pendant in the form of a Cretan wild goat, the agrimi (**59**, *right*), very like a Cretan seal-impression of the eighteenth century BC (**60**). The three discs which hang from it bring it into relation with our no. 1. Second, a tantalising fragment with lion's heads (**59**, *centre*); and, in the third place, a very Egyptian-looking figure of a falcon which is not true Egyptian but a Cretan imitation (**59**, *left*). It had a stone inlay (probably diopside) which associates it with the rings nos. 13–16. And, finally (**61**) an ornament in the shape of a bee, decorated with filigree and granulation: a poor relation (but not so very poor at that) of the bee-pendant from Mallia (**14**). These four pieces were acquired in 1875 and 1876 and could well come from the Chrysolakkos tomb.

The Greek island of Kythera, off the coast of Sparta, was the site of a Cretan colony, from which comes a gold necklace of palm-leaves with pendant discs (**62**), which reminds us both of the gold beads no. 11 and of the pectoral ornament no. 3, and so brings two elements of the Treasure into relationship with each other. Parallels to the latest elements in the Treasure have already been noted from the Royal Shaft Graves at Mycenae, which contain much Cretan material.

59 Three gold pendants in the British Museum; from Crete. Left, a Cretan version of an Egyptian falcon, with cloisonné inlay; centre, a heraldic arrangement of lions' heads (incomplete); right, a Cretan wild goat, with pendant discs, like ills. 17 and 22.

60 Cretan seal-impression of a wild goat, from Phaestos.
61 Gold ornament from Crete in the form of a bee. British Museum.
62 A gold necklace, from the island of Kythera, composed of palm-leaf beads like illus. 32, with disc-pendants like ills. 17 and 22.

It would be satisfying to be able to follow this lavish and imaginative tradition into later ages. But in fact events took another turn. With the occupation of Knossos about 1450 BC by Mycenaeans from the Greek mainland, and the subsequent domination of the Aegean area by Mycenaeans in place of Cretans, the taste arose for a different kind of jewellery, more formalised and considerably less elaborate. But that is another story.

Appendix

A catalogue of the Aegina Treasure, abbreviated from *BSA* lii (1957), 42–57, with a few corrections and additions.

1. A gold pendant ornament, 6 cm. high, composed of an upper plate of sheet-gold worked in relief, and backed by a flat sheet of gold. The plates are joined not (as one might expect) by soldering, but by folding the edges together.

A man stands, his body facing the front, his legs in profile to the right. In either hand he holds by the neck a goose and behind him are two sacred bull's horns (?). The horns rest on three lotus-flowers springing from upturned portions of a horizontal ground-line, on which the man stands. He wears a tall ornamental head-dress, large circular earrings, spiral bracelets on his wrists and upper arms, a tightly fitting tunic, shorts, and a tight belt with an embroidered tassel. From the relief hang five gold discs, decorated in a system of raised dots forming a circle with a central point and attached by a long 'tail' made in the same piece and wound round itself to make a loop.

A hole runs sideways along the top of the head-dress, so that the piece could hang from a cord or a wire.

(Illus. 11, **63***) BMC Jewellery* no. 762

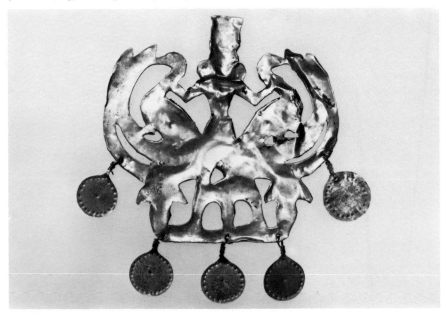

63 The back of the pendant, illus. 11.

2. Four almost identical gold ornaments, 6.5 cm. wide, making two identical pairs. Made, like no. 1 above, in relief they differ in being reversible; the back (they are symmetrical) is identical with the front. Within an embossed ring in the form of a two-headed snake are a pair of greyhounds face to face and, below them, a pair of monkeys back to back. The greyhounds stand with their muzzles joining, and each raises one forefoot so that the paw touches the opposing paw of his counterpart; they have separately-made collars, leads, and tails of wire, the leads being threaded through cornelian beads; below their raised forepaws is a barrel-shaped cornelian bead threaded on wire. Below each, supporting on its head a foreleg of the dog above it, sit two monkeys back to back, apparently eating. In front of each monkey is an object curving away from it, which supports the hind-legs of a greyhound. Seven circular discs and seven figures of flying owls are attached alternately by chains to the outer circumference of the ring. The owls are embossed and are like the main element, hollow and reversible. At the inner end of the chains for the owls is an elongated cornelian bead; at the outer end of every chain is a smaller spherical bead of the same material.

(Illus. **17, 64, 65***) BMC Jewellery* nos. 763–6

3. A gold embossed ornament with a flat back soldered to it, 11 cm. long. At either end of a curved plate with raised rims is a human head in profile. The eyes and eyebrows were originally inlaid, probably with lapis lazuli. Ears and hair are rendered in great detail, the hair being combed back and terminating in two curls on the neck; they should probably be regarded as falling on either side of the head. On top of each head is a ring for suspension, and below the piece hang ten discs like those of no. 1 above, but undecorated.

(Illus. **22***) BMC Jewellery* no. 761

4. A gold ornament, of total length 8.5 cm. The principal element consists of a lion's head with two upright pointed ears, made separately, and is pierced on either side for suspension. The collar is decorated in filigree with circles and tangent lines. A pin runs inside from the top of the lion's head to the bottom of a hollow receptacle of semicircular outline, decorated with three pairs of ribbed lines. From wire spirals on the collar hang chains, to which are attached four pendants; two represent eggs and two are in the form of flying birds, probably duck, modelled front and back like the owls of no. 2. From the receptacle hang three more birds like the upper pair, but not identical. An object in some perishable material has been lost between the lion's head and the receptacle; the pin would have run through the centre to secure it.

(Illus. **25***) BMC Jewellery* no. 746

5. A gold pendant, 6 cm. long, consisting of two figures of owls on chains, as in no. 2, suspended from a barrel-shaped cornelian bead, capped with gold. At the top end of the bead is a small ring for attachment. From an elaborate ornament like nos. 2 and 4.

(Illus. **27***) BMC Jewellery* no. 752

6. Fifty-four identical gold plaques, 4 cm. in diameter, consisting of a convex boss decorated with a rosette by means of impressed dots, having a raised border, and surrounded by eight connected spirals. The border and the spirals are decorated with impressed transverse lines. Each plaque is pierced at four points on the circumference.

(Illus. **28***) BMC Jewellery* nos. 692–745

7. Two gold diadems, 37.5 cm. and 48 cm. long respectively, the ends of which are drawn out and made into loops.

(Illus. **30***, centre* and *right) BMC Jewellery* nos. 683, 684

8. A gold band, 39.7 cm. long, decorated by means of raised dots with two lines of returning spirals between two straight lines. Nine small holes are pierced in one end.

(Illus. **30***, left) BMC Jewellery* no. 691

9. A number of thin gold bands, broken from longer bands, about 1.5 cm. wide. The ends, where preserved, are pierced.

BMC Jewellery nos. 685–90

10. A heavy gold bracelet, 7 cm. in diameter.

(Illus. **31***) BMC Jewellery* no. 767

11. Two sets of double-sided hollow gold beads in the shape of palm-leaves. Width 1.8 cm.

(Illus. **32***) BM* nos. 758A and 759A

12. Eleven beads in the form of a right hand holding a woman's breast; 1 × 1.5 cm. Three are of cornelian; three of lapis lazuli, and five of gold.

(Illus. **33***) BM* no. 756A

13. A gold ring, 2 cm. in diameter. The outer surface is inlaid with lapis lazuli, which serves as a background for an oblique meander pattern in gold.

(Illus. **35***) BMC Finger Rings* no. 693

14. A gold ring, 1.9 cm. in diameter. The outer surface is inlaid with two parallel rows of lapis lazuli; the bezel is a reef knot, also of gold, inlaid with two rows of lapis lazuli.

(Illus. **35***) BMC Finger Rings* no. 691

15. A ring composed of a solid gold hoop, flat inside and rounded outside, with an oval bezel set at right angles. Diameter 2.1 cm. The bezel has a semicircular indentation at either side, and is inlaid, like nos. 13 and 14, with lapis lazuli in gold cloisons.

(Illus. **35***) BMC Finger Rings* no. 690

64, 65 Two gold earrings from the Treasure. They can be compared with illus. 17.

16. A gold ring in the form of a thin plate, with both edges turned outwards. Diameter 2.3 cm. The groove so formed is filled with lapis lazuli, fluted diagonally.

(Illus. **35***) BMC Finger Rings* no. 692

17. The bezel and part of the hoop of a ring of thin gold foil. The bezel is a convex oval, decorated with cross-hatched lines; the hoop is grooved down the middle.

(Illus. **35***) BMC Finger Rings* no. 888

18. Five plain gold rings with open ends, about 3 cm. in diameter.

(Illus. **38***) BMC Jewellery* no. 751

19. A necklace consisting of: (1) twenty-six gold collared beads with circular depressions; (2) six small spherical and biconical gold beads; (3) twenty-five pointed-oval gold pendants on chains.

(Illus. **40***, top) BM* no. 753A

20. A necklace consisting of: (1) eighty gold melon-shaped beads, of which seven (three at the left and four at the right) are collared; (2) fifteen green jasper pendants with a gold cap at one end, representing acorns.

(Illus. **40***, centre) BM* no. 754A

21. A necklace consisting of: (1) 166 cornelian beads of spherical or slightly biconical form; (2) one cornelian oval bead; (3) fifteen cornelian barrel beads; (4) three cornelian cylindrical beads with engraved encircling lines; (5) three amethyst triple spacing beads of anygdaloid shape.

(Illus. **40***, bottom) BM* no. 760A

22. A flanged disc-bead of rock-crystal, perforated diametrically.

(Illus. **41***) BMC Jewellery* no. 757

23. A gold one-handled cup, 9.7 cm. in diameter, with a concave offset rim, embossed with a rosette at the bottom and with spirals running round the bowl. The handle is now missing.

(Illus. **42**, **43***) BMC Jewellery* no. 768

Bibliography and Notes

GENERAL

Complete publications of the Treasure
(1) A.J. Evans, *JHS* xiii (1892–3), 195–226
(2) F.H. Marshall, *BMC Jewellery*, xviii–xx and 51–56.
(3) R.A. Higgins, *BSA* lii (1957), 42–57.
The rings also published in F.H. Marshall, *BMC Finger Rings*, 115, 145

CHAPTER 1 A TREASURE IS BOUGHT

No bibliography required.

CHAPTER 2 INVESTIGATIONS, 1893–1957

First publication of Treasure: A.J. Evans, *JHS* xiii (1892–3), 195–226.
Vases in Ashmolean: nos. AE 299–302.
Vases in British Museum: *Catalogue of Vases* i, pt. i (1925), nos. A 1091, A 1092.
Excavation by Stais: *AE* 1895, 252
Excavation by Keramopoullos: *AE* 1910. 178, 183.
Investigations by Harland: J.P. Harland, *Prehistoric Aigina*. Paris, 1925, 24.
Excavations by Welter: G. Welter, *Aigina*. Berlin, 1938.
Marshall's views: *BMC Jewellery*, xviii–xx.
Myres's views: *Antiquity* xxv (1951), 70.
Seventh century?: P. Demargne, *La Créte dédalique*. Paris, 1947, 126. G. Becatti, *Oreficerie antiche dalle Minoiche alle Barbariche*. Rome, 1955, 38. *American Journal of Archaeology* lxvi (1962), 182–4.
Phoenician?: H.L. Lorimer, *Homer and the Monuments*. London, 1950, 71.
Excavation of Mallia tomb: *Etudes Crétoises* vii, 25–59.
Views of present author: *BSA* lii (1957), 42–57.

CHAPTER 3 DESCRIPTION OF THE TREASURE

No. 1. *BMC Jewellery* no. 762.
Cretan dress: S. Hood, *The Minoans*. London, 1971, 94–6.
Pin from Mycenae: Marinatos and Hirmer, pl. 200, left.
Mallia lotus, bee-jewel and leaf: *Etudes Crétoises* vii, pls. 22, 66 and 67. Marinatos and Hirmer, pl. 13, bottom (bee jewel only).
Egyptian wall painting: British Museum, *Introductory Guide to the Egyptian Collections*. London, 1964, 15, fig. 6.
No. 2. *BMC Jewellery* nos. 763–6.
Mallia bird: *Etudes Crétoises* vii, pl. 67.3.
Thera fresco: S. Marinatos, *Thera* v (1972), pl. K.
Cretan monkeys: Seager, *Mochlos*, fig. 11. Xanthoudides, pl. 15, no. 1026. *CMS* ii pt. 5, no. 297.
Egyptian pectoral: A. Wilkinson, *Ancient Egyptian Jewellery*. London, 1971, pl. xvii and col. pl. ii.

No. 3. *BMC Jewellery* no. 761.
Sphinx: Boardman, *Gems and Rings*, pl. 30.
Human head: ibid. fig. 53.
No. 4. *BMC Jewellery* no. 746.
Mallia axe-head: *Etudes Crétoises*, i, pl. 32. Marinatos and Hirmer, pl. 68.
No. 5. *BMC Jewellery* no. 752.
No. 6. *BMC Jewellery* nos. 692–745.
Similar patterns: Karo, *Schachtgräber*, pl. 39. Mylonas, *Grave Circle B*, pl. 182.
No. 7. *BMC Jewellery* nos. 683–4.
Diadems of this form, but embossed: Karo, *Schachtgräber*, pls. 36–9. Mylonas, *Grave Circle B*, pls. 21 and 159.
No. 8. *BMC Jewellery* no. 691.
Decoration with raised dots: Seager, *Mochlos*, figs. 8, 9 etc. Xanthoudides, pl. 57.
Double spiral pattern: Evans, *Palace*, iii, 295, fig. 193. Karo, *Schachtgräber*, pls. 55 and 174.
No. 9. *BMC Jewellery* nos. 685–90.
Similar bands: Seager, *Mochlos*, figs. 8 and 10. *Etudes Crétoises* vii, pl. 65. Mylonas, *Grave Circle B*, pl. 59.
No. 10. *BMC Jewellery* no. 767.
Egyptian bracelet: A. Wilkinson, *Ancient Egyptian Jewellery*. London, 1971, pl. 74C.
No. 11. BM nos. 758A and 759A.
Similar beads: Mylonas, *Grave Circle B*, pl. 181.
No. 12. BM no. 756A.
Figurine-vase: Marinatos and Hirmer, pl. 10 top.
Ur beads: C.L. Woolley, *Ur Excavations* ii. London and Philadelphia, 1939, passim.
No. 13. *BMC Finger Rings* no. 693.
Ring from Ur: Woolley, *op. cit.* pl. 138.
Tomb with inlaid ring: *AAA* i (1968), 254. At Poros, near Heraklion.
Cretan vase: Seager, *Mochlos*, fig. 31.
No. 14. *BMC Finger Rings* no. 691.
No. 15. *BMC Finger Rings* no. 690.
Boeotian shield: *JHS* xiii (1892–3), 213–218.
Double-axe on vase: Marinatos and Hirmer pl. 81.
No. 16. *BMC Finger Rings* no. 692.
No. 17. *BMC Finger Rings* no. 888.
Somewhat similar rings: E.H. Hall, *Excavations in Eastern Crete. Sphoungaras.* Philadelphia, 1912, 69, fig. 43 A & B.
No. 18. *BMC Jewellery* no. 751.
Fresco of bead: Evans, *Palace* i, 312, fig. 231 and 526, fig. 383.
No. 19. BM no. 753A.
No. 20. BM no. 754A.
No. 21. BM no. 760A.
Similar amethyst beads: Evans, *Palace* iv, col. pl. xxxiv.
No. 22. *BMC Jewellery* no. 757.
Similar beads: Seager, *Mochlos*, fig. 41 and pl. 10.
No. 23. *BMC Jewellery* no. 768.
Gold Cup: O. Picard & J. P. Sodini, *Collection Hélène Stathatos*, iv, Athens, 1971, pl. iii, no. St.700.
Silver cup: Evans, *Palace* ii, 387, fig. 221a.

Gold goblet: Marinatos and Hirmer, pl. 192, top.
Pottery cup: *Phylakopi*, 134, fig. 106 and pl. 27.3.
Female statuettes: Reynold Higgins, *Minoan and Mycenaean Art*. London, 1967, ills. 3, 22, 167.
Frescoes from,Thera: *Thera* vii, Colour Plates A–K.

CHAPTER 4   MORE INVESTIGATIONS, 1959–77

Welter's posthumous book: G. Welter, *Aigina*. Athens, 1962; in Greek.
Gold suit for a child: E. Vermeule, *Greece in the Bronze Age*. Chicago and London, 1964, pl. x.

CHAPTER 5   WHAT REALLY HAPPENED?

Cretan pottery at Aegina: Welter, *Archäologischer Anzeiger*, 1925, 319, fig. 4; 1937, 23.
Cretan potters-wheel discs: P. Warren, *Antiquity* xliii (1969), 224–7.
Pausanias on Aegina: Pausanias, *Guide to Greece* (translated by Peter Levi). Harmondsworth, 1971, i, 201.
Tomb-robber's hoard from Mycenae: *BSA* xxxix (1938–9), 65–87.
Tomb-robber's hoard from Tiryns: *Athenische Mitteilungen* lv (1930), 119–40.
Egyptian tomb-robber: C. Aldred, *Jewels of the Pharaohs*. London, 1971, 7.

CHAPTER 6   THE CRETAN GOLDSMITH

This chapter is based largely on R.A. Higgins, *Greek and Roman Jewellery*. London, 1961.
For further technical information, see H. Hoffmann and P.F. Davidson, *Greek Gold*. Mainz, 1965; C. Aldred, *Jewels of the Pharaohs*. London, 1971.

North Syrian gold: K.R. Maxwell-Hyslop, *Western Asiatic Jewellery*. London, 1971, 230.
Text from Mari: *Syria* xx (1939), 111.
Egyptian imports from Crete: S. Hood, *The Minoans*. London, 1971, 125.
Moulds: *Bulletin of the Museum of Fine Arts, Boston* lxv (1967), 19–31.
Wire: A. Oddy, 'The Production of Gold Wire in Antiquity', *Gold Bulletin*, 1977, 79.
Stone mould for ring: *BMC Jewellery* no. 609.
Mochlos jewellery: Seager, *Mochlos*, passim.
First Palace Period jewellery: R.A. Higgins *Greek and Roman Jewellery*. London, 1961, 63, figs. 8, 10.
Mallia jewellery: *Etudes Crétoises* vii, 25–59.
Gold standing lion from Knossos: Evans, *Palace* iii, 412, fig. 275A.
Goat in British Museum: *BMC Jewellery*, no. 815.
Seal impression of goat, from Phaestos: *CMS* ii, pt. v, no. 255.
Fragment with lions' heads in British Museum: *BMC Jewellery* no. 816.
Falcon in British Museum: *BMC Jewellery* no. 817.
Bee in British Museum: *BMC Jewellery* no. 1239.
Necklace from Kythera: J.N. Coldstream and G.L. Huxley, *Kythera*. London, 1972, pl. 84.

List of Illustrations

Index